Mario Gomboli
With Giorgio Chiozzi
THE MOST AMAZING ANIMALS!

COURAGE
B O O K S
AN IMPRINT OF RUNNING PRESS
PHILADELPHIA • LONDON

Original Italian-language edition
© Mario Gomboli
NUOVI RECORD BESTIALI
Translated by Martin Mayes

English-language edition
© 1998

ISBN 0-7624-0468-X
Library of Congress Cataloging in Publication Number 98-73665

First American edition published in 1998 by
Courage Books, an imprint of
Running Press Book Publishers
125 South Twenty - second Street
Philadelphia, PA 19103-4399

INTRODUCTION

Beyond the faintest shadow of a doubt, right at this very moment,
someone, somewhere is just about
to say that the cheetah is the fastest living creature alive
(it can travel at speeds as high as 70 mph) and that the kangaroo can jump a full 30 feet
(that's almost twice the distance an Olympic champion can manage!).
But did you know that the biggest animals ever to live wasn't a dinosaur but a whale;
that the scarab beetle is a prize weight-lifter;
and that the flea is a champion high-jumper?
There are many more animals that are just as amazing.
Some are surprisingly fast or strong, while others are just zanier, uglier,
or smaller than any other animals alive!
Come to think of it, animals aren't the only amazing creatures on this planet.
Read on, and you may even discover some stunning facts about plants
that will amaze your family and friends. You never know what weird, strange,
or wondrous creatures you'll encounter next!

RECORD EARS

Ears come in all shapes and sizes, and the world is full of animals who are extremely proud of their unique method of hearing. . . . Whether large or small, silky smooth or hairy, lend your ear to the following tribute to animal ears.

Long-eared bat

African elephant

Ailanthus silk moth

Desert fox

House mouse

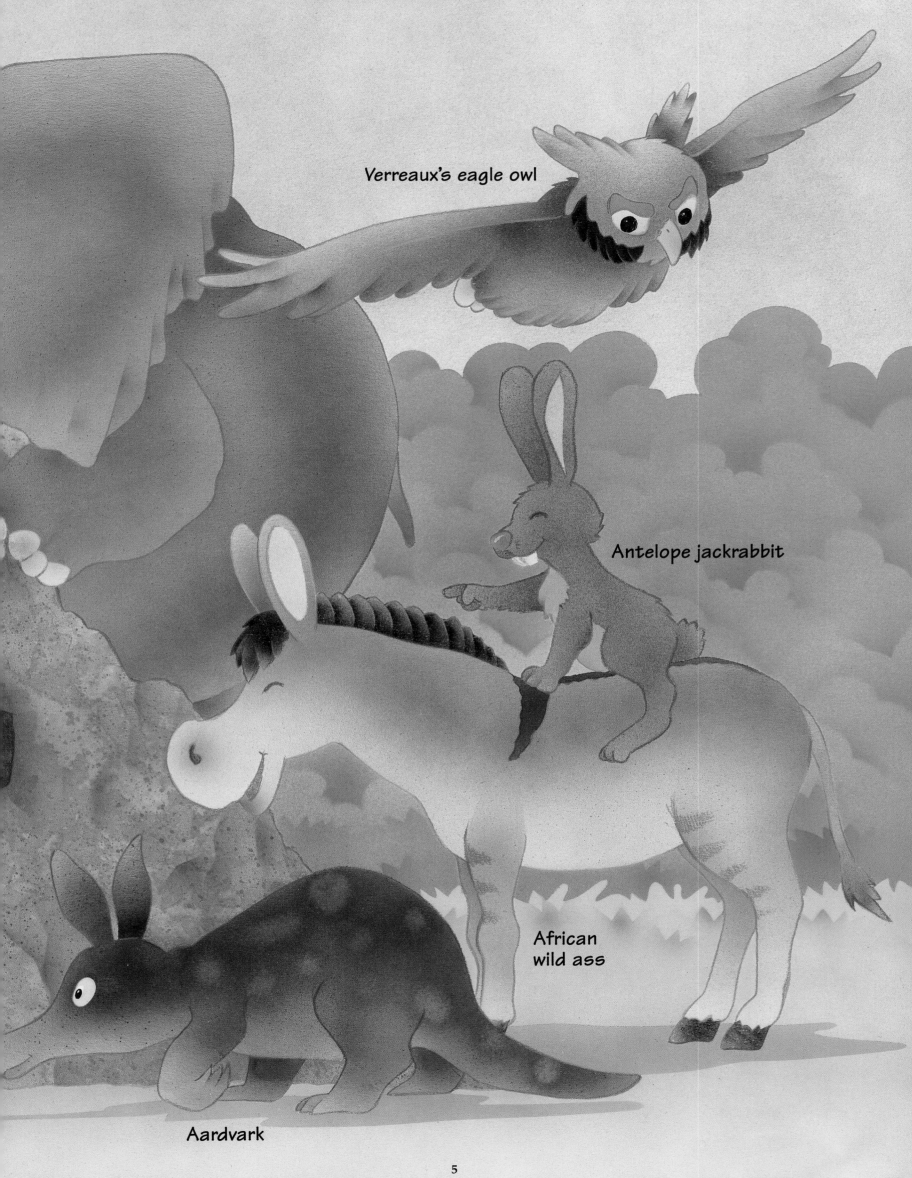

Verreaux's eagle owl

Antelope jackrabbit

African wild ass

Aardvark

THE BIGGEST

The biggest ears flapping about on dry land belong to the AFRICAN ELEPHANT. If you put its right and left ears together they are bigger than a bedsheet. When they move they create a sort of mini whirlwind that is strong enough to dislodge the cloud of parasitic insects that torment this poor animal. This is only one of their ears' functions. They also frighten enemies. When the elephant charges, it open out its ears to make it look even bigger—as if that were really necessary!

THE MOST SENSITIVE

If, in the sandy dunes of the Sahara Desert, you ever happen to see two quivering ears sticking up, don't try to attract their attention by whistling. You will may give the poor DESERT FOX a terrible headache. This small fox, about the size of a cat, has extremely sensitive ears which help it detect the quietest rustling of a beetle's little legs (one of its favorite tasty morsels) even when several feet away. And that's why in captivity it suffers, horribly. To its sensitive ears, even the quietest house can sound noisier than a nightclub!

THE FUNNIEST

The amusing AARDVARK looks like a grayish pig with rabbit ears. But the termites of East Africa don't find it the least bit funny. The Aardvark, completely indifferent to their bites, enjoys opening up their nests and dining on all the termites it can capture with its long sticky tongue. And while it's eating, it keeps its ears pinned back and listens for any suspicious sounds—after all you never can tell who might jump out at you during dinner!

THE MOST SPECIALIZED

The LONG-EARED BAT lives up to its name, with ears that are three times the size of its head. In fact, this little European bat is proud of having large ears that pick up ultrasonic echoes to guide him around even when it's dark. The only problem with such big ears is that they become cold quite quickly, so the long-eared bat never goes out in bad weather. At the first sign of winter, it retreats to its cave to hibernate, wrapping its body—and most especially its ears—in the warmth of its fur-covered wings.

THE PHONIEST

Both traditional fairy tales and modern animated cartoons have nurtured the ideas that the owl is a wise, friendly animal, always ready to lend an ear to pleas for help and advice from other inhabitants of the forest.
In actual fact, other animals do their very best to stay as far away as possible from the owl's extremely sharp claws. What look like ears sticking up on the top of its head are merely small tufts of feathers designed to make the VERREAUX'S EAGLE OWL look as awesome and as frightening as possible. The ears it uses for listening are actually hidden openings in its skull that can close to make itself deaf to the rest of the world!
To further heighten its terrifying appearance, this bird of prey also sports eyebrows and side whiskers also made of feathers.

THE MOST LOVABLE

So much for the owl being wise. What about our idea of the hare? With its pointed face, twitching nose, soft fur, and long ears it seems extremely lovable. The rabbit is an extremely defenseless animal and its long ears aren't merely pretty, but help it detect the slightest sign of danger. The rabbit's only way of avoiding a predator is to run. And it has four powerful legs that help it run really fast.
What better way to know when flight is necessary than to have ever-attentive ears? The ANTELOPE JACKRABBIT has ears which are more than a quarter the length of the rest of its body.

THE MOST EXTRAORDINARY

It goes without saying that all ears are able to detect sound. But those of the male AILANTHUS SILK MOTH (which originally came from China) are able to "hear" smells!
Its ears are actually huge antennae that are able to recognize the presence of interesting molecules (such as those of the female's "perfume") even when they're dispersed thinly through the air.

THE MOST FAMOUS

The common HOUSE MOUSE owes a great debt to Mickey Mouse.
Thanks to Walt Disney and his much-loved characters the mouse's round ears have become a symbol especially adored by children everywhere and nobody dares to kill these cheeky little cheese thieves. Unfortunately, cats don't watch the Disney Channel! Luckily, escape is always possible because those round ears stay tuned to catch the quiet pad of the paws of any approaching cat trying to get too close.

THE MOST UNDERAPPRECIATED

When it come to symbols, the donkey's ears would be never our first choice as the symbol of intelligence. This is in spite of the fact that the poor beast has diligently (and far from stupidly) served its thankless masters in Europe.
In Africa and Asia the donkey is believed to be close to divinity.
Just remember how Joseph and Mary escaped from Egypt on a donkey's back and that Jesus himself was warmed by a donkey's breath.
That Biblical donkey might just have been an AFRICAN WILD ASS.
Today, however, these beasts are threatened with extinction.

SPINE TINGLERS

It's not only cacti whose prickles dissuade you from wanting to give them a hug and a squeeze. There are also some animals that you might not want to pet or stroke. A few of them are a threat to humans. So beware!

Common iguana

Swordfish

Spiny ant

Stingray

Porcupine fish

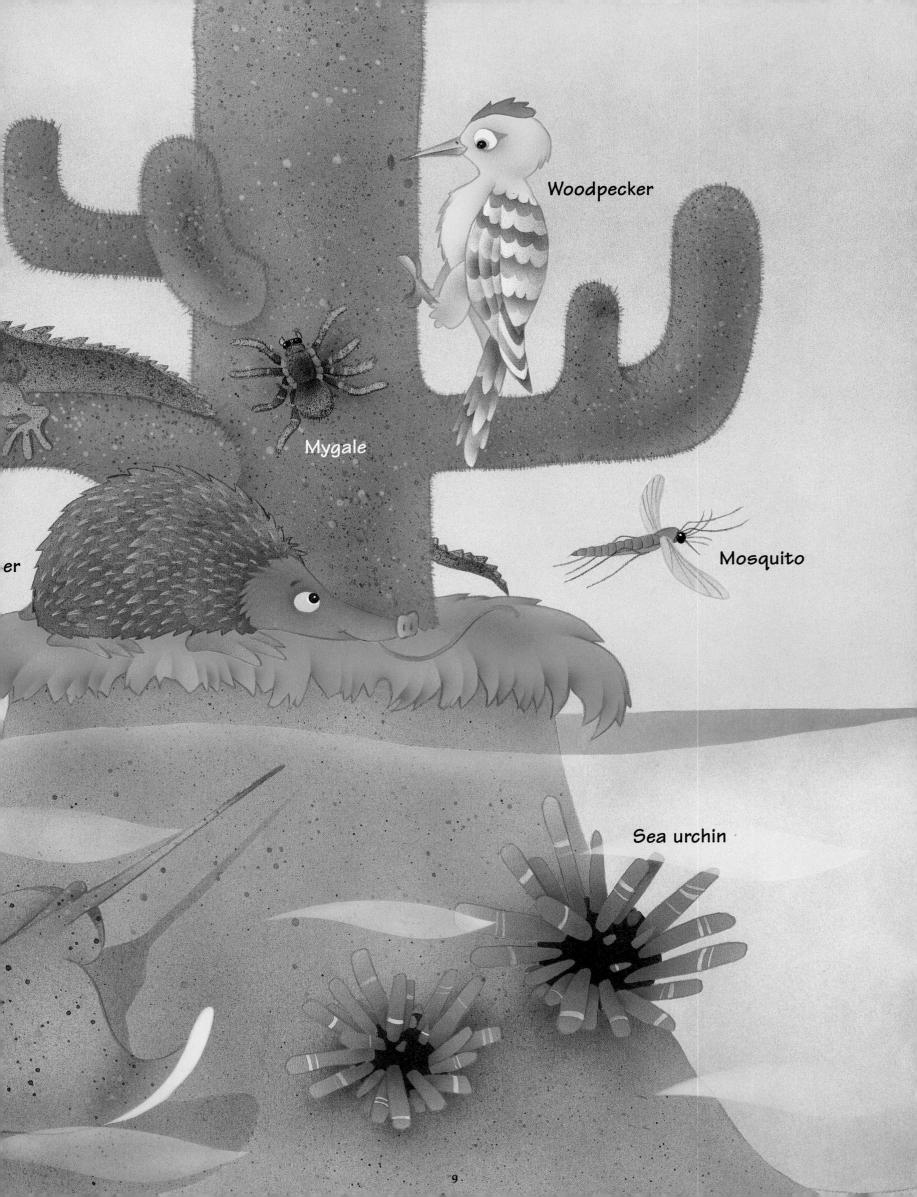

Woodpecker

Mygale

Mosquito

Sea urchin

er

9

THE MOST IRRITATING

The male MOSQUITO never bothers us at all. Only the female mosquito maddens us with her bite because she need blood to feed her eggs. The itch from a mosquito bite doesn't come from the bite itself but from an irritating substance injected during the bite which helps stimulate a greater flow of blood. This makes life so much easier for the mosquito but so much unhappier for us.

THE MOST DECEPTIVE

The SPINY ANTEATER lives in Australia. It's a small *oviparous* mammal—an animal that lays eggs but then suckles its babies on milk.

A more technical name for the spiny anteater is ECHIDNA. Echidna -comes from Greek and means spiny. Its used for other animals such as sea urchins, because they're also covered with spines. But the spines on the anteater aren't very sharp or dangerous, so relax.

But it does have one secret weapon—its back paws have a sharp poisonous talon so don't get too close!

THE MOST ALARMING

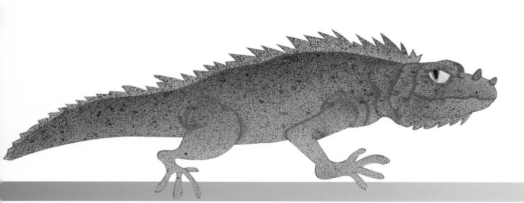

The COMMON IGUANA moves quickly through the South American forest even though it's over five feet long and weighs more than thirty pounds. It looks like a fearsome little dinosaur, with a deadly-looking row of spines along its back and under its chin. but don't panic—it's unlikely to attack because it prefers running away and its favorite food is fruit and the eggs of other animals.

THE DEADLIEST

Everybody knows that if you're wandering around in the Amazon forest and you happen to come across a hairy spider as big as your hand you need to change direction immediately. The MYGALE's sting is extremely poisonous. But if you were foolish enough to think that you could pick this spider up without touching its sting, you would be poisoned anyway. The sharp, rigid hairs that cover its body are also poisonous and can easily pierce human skin.

THE LEAST DANGEROUS

If, when walking over a coral reef, you happened to step on a RICCIO A MATITA, the only one to suffer would be the poor sea urchin. Its spines are quite the opposite of those of its European relatives—they are as big as one of your fingers, hard as a rock, and the points are gently rounded. Because of this its not able to defend itself from its enemies such as star fish and souvenir hunters, the combined efforts of which are threatening it with extinction.

THE MOST ELECTRIFYING

The STINGRAY has large fins all along both sides
of its body so it looks almost like a kite.
It doesn't need weapons for hunting since it eats only
defenseless mollusks, but to ward off its enemies it has
a tail that is long and venomous. And as if that weren't
enough, it also has an organ in its tail that generates
an electric current strong enough to give you a small
electric shock. It's probable that this is a radar rather
than a defense mechanism, but the resulting
shock is just as stunning.

THE NOISIEST

There are many types of WOODPECKERS all over the world,
and though their brightly colored plumage varies from country to country,
they all look quite similar and they all have a strong bill that can bore
through bark, into tree trunks, and even make a hole in clay.
The technique it uses is similar to that of a pneumatic drill—it bangs
its head in a frantic rhythm until it has made the hole it wants.
It seems to me that it does rather more than just peck,
wouldn't you agree? If you or I were to try to imitate
it we would get a sever headache, but the woodpecker's brain
is surrounded by a liquid that acts as a shock absorber.

THE MOST REMARKABLE

In the coral reefs carpeted with sea urchins there lives a fish
that has no fins on its belly and has a beak instead of a mouth.
It's a fat, tiny thing that's slightly egg-shaped—an appetizing
sight that attracts predators. But when they try to snap it up,
the PORCUPINE FISH turns into a totally inedible,
prickly ball. In fact, it can inflate itself up by sucking in
water so that it becomes as round as a ball and its skin
stretches to make the hundreds of spines which cover
its body stand out. It becomes so bloated it can no longer
swim but that doesn't matter; its frightened enemies
take off in a hurry.

THE MOST WANTED

While many animals are equipped with spines that they don't actually use as
weapons, the SWORDFISH isn't one of
them. It will readily attack its enemies,
be they tuna fish or fishing boats, and try
to run them through with its sharp jaw (which can be up to
three feet long). Occasionally it gets foolishly carried away and ends up
getting stuck in a boat's keel. Not that it's stupid. In fact, it's traditionally thought
to be an intelligent fish. Unfortunately for the swordfish, its flesh is prized as a
delicacy. Fishermen, not being an easily frightened lot, set out to catch it using nets that
are several miles long and can't be damaged by sword thrusts.

PREHISTORIC MAMMALS

After those large reptiles, the dinosaurs, became extinct, the Earth was taken over by a new race of warm-blooded animals. These animals came in all shapes and sizes, and their bodies were covered to varying extents with hair. From the most peaceful to the most ferocious, they had one thing in common—they were all mammals because they all fed their little ones milk.

Pyrotherium

Eobasileus

Elephas falconeri

Epigaulus

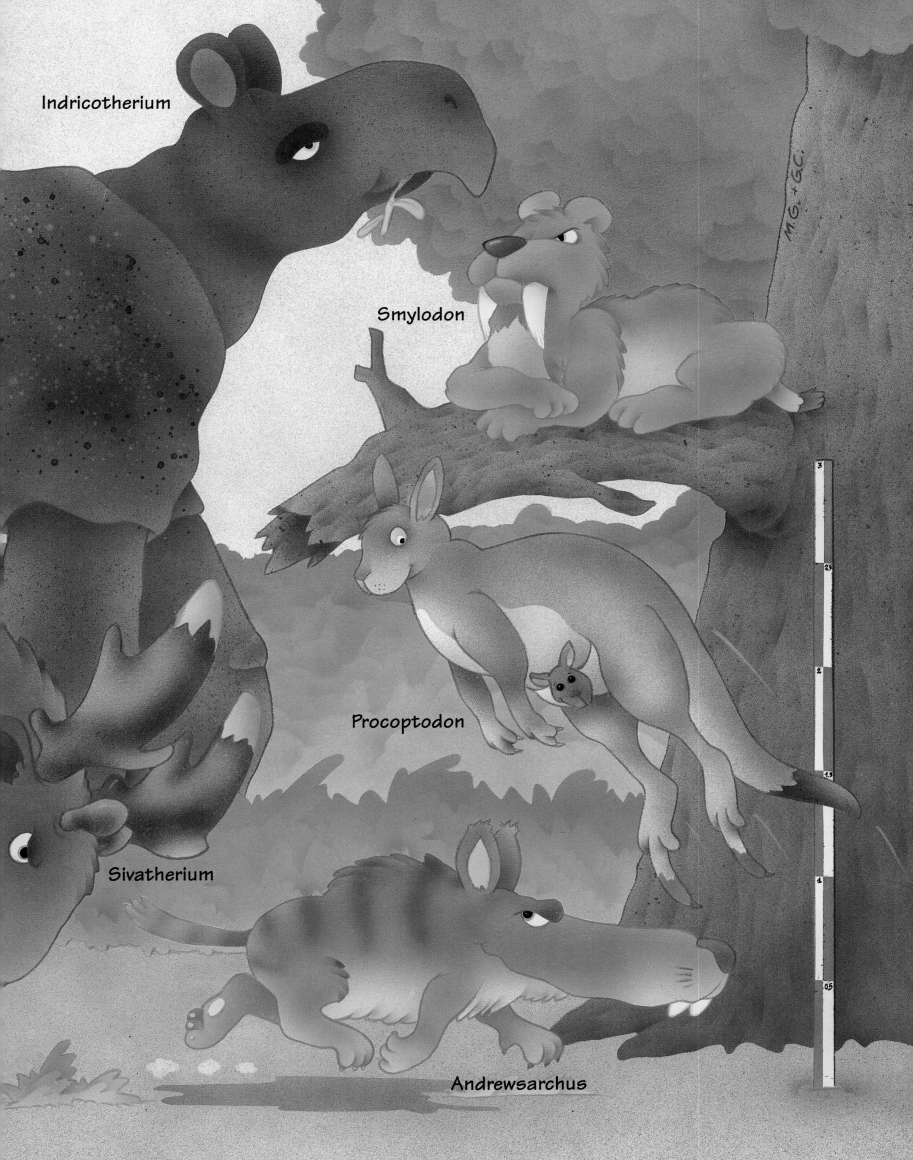

Indricotherium

Smylodon

Procoptodon

Sivatherium

Andrewsarchus

THE BIGGEST MAMMAL

Taller than a giraffe and weighing more than four elephants, the INDRICOTHERIUM is the largest mammal ever to have walked the Earth. It inhabited the vast Asian grasslands more than thirty million years ago. With its huge, soft lips it ate leaves from the highest branches (as high as twenty-five feet off the ground). It's gigantic body weighed a massive thirty tons, so it could simply squash any unwary predator who dared disturb it.

THE CUTEST

Five million years ago, sea levels fell unusually low and some elephants were able to cross over from the European continent to islands such as Sicily in the Mediterranean. When the sea levels rose again, they were stranded and soon learned that these small islands didn't have enough food to sustain them. Over years they evolved into increasingly smaller creatures. The ELEPHAS FALCONERI looked just like an elephant, but it was no bigger than a German Shepherd.

THE WEIRDEST

The EPIGAULUS was probably similar in shape, size, and habits to today's marmot. Twenty million years ago it used its strong nails to burrow holes throughout North America. So what was weird about it? It had two horns on the tip of its nose. These horns made it difficult for it to disappear down one of its burrows without being noticed. Because none of today's rodents have horns, it's not clear whether they served as weapons, were used for digging, or were just "beauty spots."

THE UGLIEST

With the body of a hairy pig, a short stumpy trunk (it was a relative of the early elephant), feet as flat as pancakes, and an anteater's tongue, the PYROTHERIUM was not a pretty sight. Thirty million years ago, this mammal lived in the South American jungle. It probably used its strange mouth for digging up plants and roots in the mud.

THE NIMBLEST

If you've ever seen a kangaroo leap, you'll find it easy to imagine what bounds its ten-foot long great-great-grandfather must have made! The PROCOPTODON lived in Australia, where it used its height to reach the tastiest leaves on the trees and carried its young around in its pouch. If it was threatened and escape proved impossible, it would defend itself from predators with the huge claws it had on its front paws or by kicking violently with the talon on its hind leg.

THE FIERCEST

The SMYLODON, a feline animal about the size of a lynx, lived in the American grasslands two million years ago. With a short tail and two sizable fangs, it was a ruthless hunter capable of ripping open the thick skin of any pachyderm with just one bite.
Unfortunately, it was too small to proceed with the kill and so, to satisfy its hunger it had to sit and wait patiently for its victim to die from loss of blood.

THE MOST HEAVILY ARMED

With a row of three pairs of horns across the top of its skull and two tusks protruding from its jaw, the EOBASILEUS, a mammal that lived on the North American plains fifty million years ago, was prepared for any opponent. These weapons on an animal the size of a rhinoceros would frighten any animal. Surprisingly, the Eobasileus was a peaceful plant-eater. We suppose that its horns were purely decorative and that its tusks were used for digging up roots.

THE LARGEST HEAD

The carnivorous mammal with the largest skull we know of was the ANDREWSARCHUS. Its skull was about three feet long, more than a third the length of the rest of its body! It lived in Mongolia at the same time as the Eobasileus. Just like today's hyenas, this weird beast preferred not to hunt but to feed on carrion (dead or decaying flesh).

THE MOST RECENT

Some cave paintings suggest that early man existed at the same time as the SIVATHERIUM. This large beast lived in North Africa and in the Himalayan foothills only eight thousand years ago. It looked a lot like a moose, though it was decidedly bigger (to the top of its shoulders it measured well over six feet). It was an aggressive animal and had both a hefty pair of antlers and a small pair of horns with rounded tips.
Today its descendants are not Canadian moose, as you might think. Strangely enough, it's the tall, long-legged giraffe. This is one of evolution's many unexpected surprises.

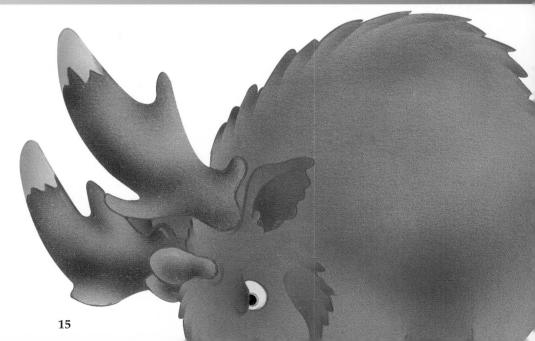

UNIQUE HORNS

Narwhal

South American
horned frog

Snail

Pronghorn

Animals sport horns and antlers of all shapes and sizes—there are big ones, small ones, smooth ones, strong ones, and really delicate ones. Some of these animals are hunted by unscrupulous men who want to kill them for their horns. Many of these animals, however, have more serious problems. Here are some of the curious facts.

Caribou

Shore lark

Horned Viper

Stag beetle

North American moose

Indian rhinoceros

THE MOST IMPRESSIVE

The NORTH AMERICAN MOOSE is the largest member of the deer family alive today. It's taller than an NBA player, heavier than a small family car, and has a pair of antlers that can weigh about forty pounds. These antlers are flat (rather like a shovel) and are deadly weapons used to fight duels to settle disagreements over territory and female mates. The females have no horns and can only look on helplessly during these disputes. When the dueling season is over, the male moose sheds its antlers. It regrows larger and even more powerful ones the following year.

THE MOST DELICATE

If you try touching the little horns on a SNAIL's head, you'll notice that they rapidly retract.
The snail's horns aren't designed for attacking enemies or defending itself.
In fact, these horns aren't even made of bone. They are tentacles made of flesh.
The snail carries its eyes on the tips of these tentacles.

THE FANCIEST

The STAG BEETLE is a very common beetle. It's about the size of one of your fingers, but a third of its length is accounted for by its horns. If a real stag had horns that were one-third its size, these horns would extend for more than six feet. The Stag beetle's "horns" are, in fact, highly developed mandibles (lower jaws). They are both practical (they have a very powerful grip) and aesthetic (Darwin thought they served to attract the female of the species, who don't have such horn-like jaws).

THE UGLIEST

In the South American swamps there lives a toad the size of a child's fist. The SOUTH AMERICAN HORNED FROG is squat and fat and covered with warts of various colors. Above its eyes it has two folds of skin which stick up and look like unsightly horns. They certainly don't help make it look any less ugly! But that's our human opinion. The female toads apparently find it extremely attractive.

THE RAREST

Some animals, such as the moose, shed their horns every year. Others keep the same pair all their lives. Then there's the PRONGHORN, a small antelope which lives on the west coast of North America, whose horns are hollow. Much like gloves, these horns fit onto a bony stump on the top of its head and come off every year. They don't break off at the base, but peel off and regrow the following year. No other animal can boast horns like this.

THE MOST SPECIALIZED

The CARIBOU is a type of deer that lives in the coldest part of North America. It feeds on grass and roots, but in these areas they are often covered by a layer of frozen snow. We believe that's why one of the two branches on its horns has a large, flat growth on the front. Much like a shovel, it seems perfectly designed for shifting snow. This is the most plausible explanation we have for the asymmetrical shape of its strange looking horns.

THE SOFTEST

What use could a lovely, easy-going bird have for a pair of horns? None, of course. The horns of the SHORE LARK (which can be found all over Europe) aren't true horns at all. They're soft, delicate black feathers. When the lark gets excited, these feathers stand on end and look just like horns.

THE MOST DANGEROUS

In your wanderings across the rocky parts of Eastern Europe, you might come across the HORNED VIPER. Its got a little horn covered with flaky skin on the tip of its nose, but you needn't worry about that. It's just a harmless decoration that won't hurt you. What you do need to worry about is the poison in its teeth. When the viper is big (and it can grow to almost three feet in length), its bite can be deadly!

THE MOST LEGENDARY

In ancient times, the tusk of the NARWHAL was thought to be the horn of the fabled unicorn (a horse with a single horn in the middle of its forehead). This marine mammal is a relative of the dolphin and it lives in the waters of the Arctic Circle. Its upper tooth can grow dramatically up to ten feet in length. It pierces the upper lip and twists round and round on itself.

THE MOST PRECIOUS

The INDIAN RHINOCEROS is about the size of a van. The small horn on the tip of its nose is nothing more than a tuft of hairs stuck together, and it serves very little purpose. Yet there are those who believe that a powder made from this horn is a magic cure for all sorts of ills. Because of this, the Indian rhinoceros has been hunted to the verge of extinction.

FIRST CLASS SLEEPERS

Giraffe

Dolphin

Chimpanzee

Slow loris

Flying fox

Armadi

Maybe they don't have soft mattresses, pillows, and sheets, but animals need to sleep just like us. Whether curled up in their nests or snug in a cave, animals need to rest in order to function. In fact, some of their sleeping habits are very strange! It all depends on how they're made and what they have to do survive.

Arabian camel

Swift

Brown bear

Dormouse

THE SLEEPIEST

The DORMOUSE is thought to spend most of its time asleep—a lazy-bone's dream existence. But the truth of the matter is that this tiny rodent spends its nights busily looking for food. The dormouse earned its lazy reputation by sleeping all day and hibernating during the winter. When it hibernates it doesn't go into a long, undisturbed sleep like some other animals. The poor animal is often quite restless, shifting its furry tail (which doubles as a blanket) and waking up occasionally to nibble on the odd snack.

THE MOST RESTLESS

The BROWN BEAR also hibernates during the winter, but its sleep is far from peaceful. In the autumn it eats continuously to fatten itself up, then it goes off to a cave to sleep for several months. It survives mostly thanks to all the fat it has accumulated, but every so often it will wake up to hunt for something to eat. The bear also gives birth and suckles its young during this period of hibernation, for caves provide them with the necessary warmth and safety.

THE MOST COMFORTABLE

The CHIMPANZEE likes a comfortable place to sleep. When it gets drowsy it begins to prepare a bed for itself; it collects leaves, weaves twigs together, and bends and ties branches. When the chimp has finally finished, it lays down to sleep. The next morning it abandons the bunk without a further thought. After all, it won't be much trouble making another one when evening comes.

THE LEAST COMFORTABLE

The SLOW LORIS is a small primate (about the size of a cat) that lives in the forests of Sri Lanka. During the night it moves slowly from one branch to another. On the ground it moves slower still! Only when it gets wind of something tasty to eat (such as an insect or reptile) does it finally leap into action in order to catch its prey. At dawn it begins (very slowly, of course) to look for a safe branch where it can shut its eyes, hang its head, and enjoy a well-deserved rest.

THE MOST RELAXED

The ARABIAN CAMEL might like to sleep lying on its back, just like a puppy begging to have its tummy scratched. But this position is impractical because of its hump.
So, at the end of a journey across the desert, the camel folds its legs underneath it body and lays its head on a soft cushion of sand. Only then does it close its eyes (which are protected by thick eyelashes) and close its nostrils so that it doesn't breathe in any very fine grains of desert sand.

THE MOST TWISTED

The GIRAFFE usually sleeps with its very long legs drawn up underneath it, just like the camel. This isn't surprising because they're distant cousins. The only problem is that the giraffe can't roll up its long neck like a snake because its neck has only seven large vertebrae, and it can't stretch it out in front of its body because its neck is too long. Besidez, if were to stretch its head out like the camel, some elephant would be sure to stumble over it, and that wouldn't be nice for either of them! And can you imagine it sleeping with its head and neck erect like some skyscraper? It would stick out for any hungry predator on the prowl looking for an easy catch such as an animal lost in sleep. That's why the giraffe sleeps with its neck arched into the air and it's nose resting on the ground.

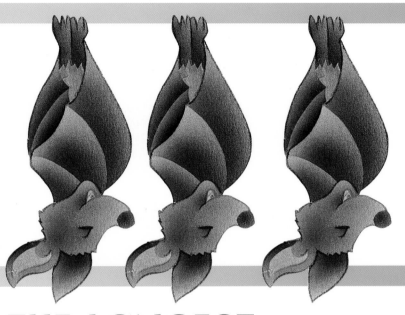

THE JUMPIEST

Like most bats, the FLYING FOX sleeps by day hanging upside down in groups of a thousand or more. In order to get a proper rest in this position you need to be able to sleep deeply without ever relaxing too much and losing your grip. Nature has equipped this animal with a conditioned reflex which makes it tense its claws continuously during its sleep, so much so that it's only possible to pull the flying fox off its perch if you wake it up first.

THE LONGEST

The South American ARMADILLO's body is covered with strong plates to protect it from attacks by predators. As a further defense it digs deep burrows in the ground and comes out only at night, avoiding the full moon whenever possible. Being so cautious allows it to sleep long hours, up to twenty hours at a stretch! That's a record for a mammal.

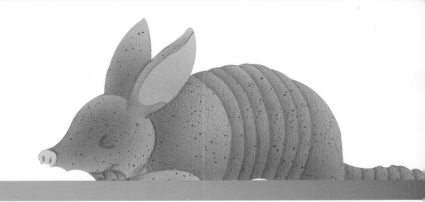

THE BRIEFEST

The SWIFT sometimes flies thousands of miles without a break. When its flying over the sea there aren't places where it can stop to rest, so the swift sleeps while flying. It takes short naps that only last a few minutes each. That way it doesn't lose altitude or its sense of direction.

THE MOST UNUSUAL

DOLPHINS are mammals and that means they have to surface at regular intervals to breathe. If they were to fall asleep underwater they would sink to the bottom of the sea and drown. But sleep is essential for survival. So the dolphin has learned to let only half of its brain go to sleep at any one time. First the left hemisphere has a rest, and then the right hemisphere takes a turn. I'll bet this is the most remarkable sleeping arrangement in the whole animal kingdom!

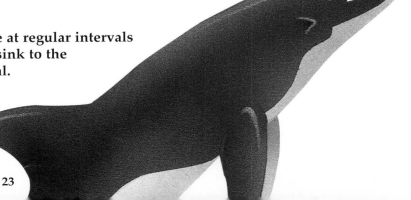

MAGNIFICENT FLYERS

From the Greek legend of Icarus onward, man has dreamed of being able to fly. While we've created machines that fly, all human attempts to imitate the flight of birds have failed miserably. For their part, animals have never stopped developing ever more sophisticated, ever more brilliant, and ever more unusual flying techniques.

Ballooning spider

Wandering Albatross

Flying fish

E

morphodon

Flying squirrel

Common Pipistrelle

Flying lizzard

Hummingbird

Dragonfly

THE EARLIEST FLIGHT

Millions of years before the dinosaur, the DRAGONFLY flew over stagnant ponds and backwaters. Scientists think it looked exactly like the dragonfly we know today, with four iridescent wings and a rainbow colored body divided into segments. It moved in rapid jerks above the surface of the water and could hover in midair like a helicopter. Its rapidly moving wings would hum like those of the modern-day dragonfly. But we suspect the noise it made was much louder, for the dragonfly's grandfather (called MEGANEURA) had a wingspan of over two feet—the same wingspan of modern pigeons!

THE MOST MYSTERIOUS

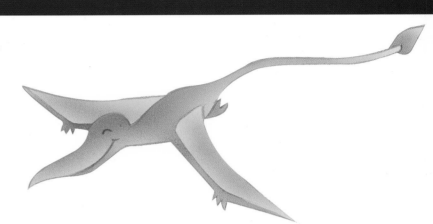

Two hundred million years ago some reptiles decided that the ground was becoming a bit too crowded and began to grow a fold of skin between the toes of their hind feet so that they could fly. The first flying reptile we know of is the EUDIMORPHODON, which was not much bigger than the Meganeura. We just can't imagine how these flying reptiles, with their short legs and extremely long tails, ever managed to take off!

THE MOST FEARLESS

Reptiles that fly no longer exist, but the FLYING DRAGON certainly does try! This little lizard of the Indonesian forests has a fold of skin on both sides of its body that is supported by two extra ribs grown specifically for that purpose. It lives high up in the trees and, when it sees a really appetizing insect, it leaps into the air with the fearlessness of a parachutist. The two folds of skin open out like wings, allowing the flying dragon to glide to the ground.

THE MOST ADORABLE

The flying dragon's technique has been copied by the FLYING SQUIRREL, which has furry folds of skin between its forelegs and hind legs. With this personal kite, the squirrel is able to fly for well over fifty feet, allowing it to move from tree to tree in pursuit of juicy fruits without being attacked by predators. The flying squirrel is the size of a cat and lives in the forests of South Asia; but there are many others that are smaller in size (some even as small as a mouse) and can be found all over the world.

THE MOST UNIQUE

The only flying mammal is the bat. Unlike a bird wings, bat wings are membranous; it's fingers are extremely long and are joined by a thin membrane of skin extending from its upper arm all the way to its feet. Even though it has a very light skeleton, it's still too heavy to just glide. To stay in the air, the bat has to flap its wings furiously without stopping. As you can imagine, this is hard work, especially for the COMMON PIPISTRELLE, Europe's smallest (it's about the size of a human hand) and most common bat.

THE MOST CAUTIOUS

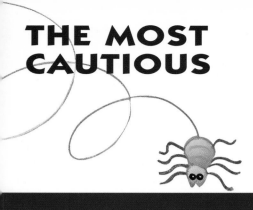

Everybody knows that spiders can't fly, but the young BALLOON SPIDER comes awfully close! It spins a very long thread (the same thread it uses to make webs) and then lets itself be carried by the wind, flying through the air. Just to be on the safe side, it keeps one end of the thread anchored to its point of departure so that it can always find its way back home.

THE SMALLEST

The HUMMINGBIRD is about one inch long and weighs less than an ounce. It lives in the Western Hemisphere from southern Alaska to the tip of South America with most dwelling along the equator in rain forests. It's not only the smallest bird alive today, but the smallest bird to have ever existed. Even its wings are the smallest of all our feathered friends and are indeed smaller than those of many insects. Their wings don't beat like those of other birds, but vibrate like those of an insect at an incredible fifty times per second! The hummingbird moves very fast, at speeds of more than thirty miles per hour. It can also remain motionless in the air like a helicopter. It flies at great speed both when moving from place to place as well as when escaping danger. When it stops to eat, it sucks nectar from flowers just like a bee. It hardly ever rests and its claws have become virtually unusable. It can perch on a branch, but it can't walk.

THE MOST AFRAID

Sometimes it's best to get as far away from a predator as possible. The FLYING FISH seems to have decided that flying is sometimes safer than swimming. Whenever it's threatened by big, greedy fish, it swims frantically to the surface with its tail throbbing like a little motor.

When it gets to the surface, it opens its wing-like pectoral fins and launches itself into the air. Once the danger has passed, the flying fish dives back down into the water.

THE LAZIEST

The WANDERING ALBATROSS is the largest airborne bird (ostriches are bigger, but they can't fly). From beak to tail its as long as an adult person, and it has a wingspan of up to thirteen feet. Thanks to this enormous wingspan, it can stay effortlessly in the air for days on end, allowing itself to be carried by the wind just like a glider. It stays on course by occasionally repositioning one of its tail feathers. The albatross's only problem is taking off, especially from land. That's why it prefers to take off from the sea, where it can run along the surface of the water and give itself an extra push or two with its webbed feet. When it has finally reached takeoff speed and has just become airborne, it draws up its feet, flaps its wings a bit to catch the wind, and sails off to hunt for little fish.

CARNIVAL TIME

Masked lovebi

Chameleon

Scaly anteater

Mandrill

Giant panda

MG·GC

Puffin

When it's time for a party, we all love to dress up and paint our faces, wear eye masks, or stick on enormous false mustaches and beards. Some animals are blessed with perfect party attire. They may have a mask or a mustache or even be able to change the color of their skin according to their mood. The following animals would make the perfect guests at your next Halloween party!

Emperor tamarin

Death's head hawk moth

Raccoon

Leaf insect

THE MOST ADORABLE

In the forests of China there lives a strange animal. Although it's the size of a bear its head is disproportionately large, and it has a beautiful black and white fur coat. It's a very picky eater and eats only the shoots of one particular kind of bamboo grass. The most striking thing about the GIANT PANDA is its eyes; they have two large black circles around them that make the panda look very sad. It does indeed have a lot of reasons to be sad. Despite the World Wildlife Federation's (the WWF) fight to save the panda and their decision to use it as their international symbol, the panda is in danger of becoming extinct because the forests where it lives and the bamboo it loves are gradually disappearing.

THE SCARIEST

When the night is darkest, there's a moth that makes its way among the creatures of the night. It's no bigger than the palm of your hand, but it can frighten anyone who's the least bit superstitious. In fact, there are people who will cross their fingers whenever they see the DEATH'S HEAD HAWK MOTH. It's actually harmless, and its only worry is avoiding mice and bats.
Unlike humans, mice and bats aren't the least bit frightened by the image of a human skull found the moth's back.

THE MOST CHANGEABLE

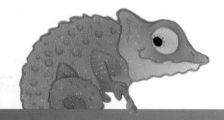

The CHAMELEON is legendary for its ability to camouflage itself by changing color. Unfortunately this is rather more legend than fact. This small animal, which lives in Africa and Madagascar, can only change the color of its skin from green to reddish brown (though you have to admit that that's quite a significant change of color). But, it doesn't really change color as a disguise, but to show whether it's feeling happy or angry.

THE BEST DISGUISE

If you ever think you're seeing a little leaf taking a walk, you're probably not going crazy. You've just met the LEAF INSECT. This animal is the most perfect example of camouflage in the animal kingdom. Its wings are a precise and complete replica of a normal leaf—right down to the veins! And that's not all, it changes color in autumn to blend in as the leaves turn from yellow to brown. When it sits on a branch it completely fools any insect-loving predator, though it does have to keep a wary eye out for vegetarians!

THE MOST ROMANTIC

The forests of Southeast Africa are crammed with millions of birds belonging to thousands of different species. One of these, the MASKED LOVEBIRDS, has a simple hood of black feathers on its head. These birds aren't very sociable and live in small groups. When they choose a mate, they remain faithful to their partners for life.

THE MOST ARMORED

In Malaysia and the South African Savannah, there lives an animal that would make any medieval knight turn green with envy. The body of the SCALY ANTEATER is protected by a flexible coat of horny scales that overlap each other just like the tiles on a roof or the metal plates on a coat of armor. When threatened the anteater rolls up into a ball so that it's both hard and inedible.

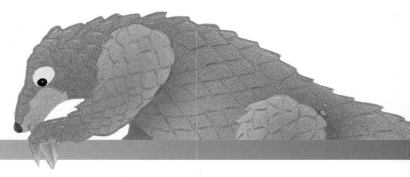

THE FUNNIEST

Now why would the EMPEROR TAMARIN, a small monkey of the Amazon jungle, grow a big mustache? It serves no practical purpose except as a built-in napkin for wiping its mouth after eating a ripe, juicy fruit. Maybe the tamarin just wants to look more attractive.

THE SNEAKIEST

Have you ever noticed that thieves in comic strips and cartoons always wear black eye masks? The raccoon also appears to wear a black mask, and that may be why many people associate them with thieves. When at home, this unfortunate creature is actually an honest type by nature, busying itself with catching fish and collecting fruit. It's true, however, that when it does wander into a big city, as happens often in North America, it rummages in trash cans and will occasionally steal the odd object from inside a house. Maybe it's learned to do this from watching cartoons.

The PUFFIN looks like it's dressed for a carnival. But despite its looks it's actually a very hard worker, spending most of its time fishing in the Atlantic Ocean. In the courting season it wears a colorful mask, a horny covering that grows on top of its beak, and sets off in search of a wife. When the fun is over, it removes its mask and goes back to its normal humdrum lifestyle.

THE MOST THEATRICAL

THE MOST COLORFUL

In the West African forests, the most beautiful animals are those with the most colorful and eye-catching masks. The face of the adult male MANDRILL, a large baboon, is blue, yellow, and red. The chief mandrill can easily be spotted because its mask is the showiest. Of course, if an intruder remains unimpressed by its display of color, the mandrill can always show off its muscles; the mandrill may only be the size of a child, but it's as strong as a grown man. And it has teeth worthy of a lion.

BURROWING BEASTS

Animals have to protect themselves against all sorts
of dangers—the heat and the cold as well as their natural
enemies. Many find unusual or creative hiding places.
What's so special about digging a hole and then
disappearing into it? Well, just try getting
into one of the holes made
by the following animals!

Rock Ptarmigan

Polar bear

Wart-hog

Elf owl

Great Indian
hornbill

Prairie dog

Scarab

Rattlesnake

Burrowing owl

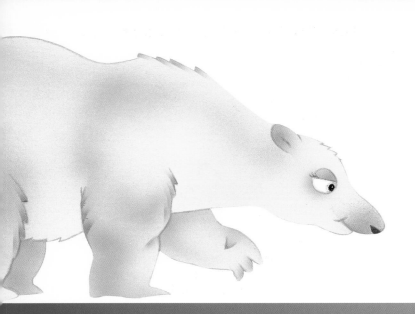

THE COLDEST BURROW

The POLAR BEAR is not as fortunate as its cousin the brown bear, which can easily find a cave in which to take shelter. When it gets too cold for the polar bear, the mother digs a tunnel in the ice where she can hole up to give birth and wean her young. She spends the whole of the long polar winter in this retreat. When spring arrives and the weather begins to get warmer (warmer, that is, by Arctic standards), the young family abandons its melting home and moves off.

THE MOST SECRET

When the time comes for it to lay its eggs, the female GREAT INDIAN HORNBILL (a member of the GREAT HORNBILL family and one of the biggest birds in Asia) withdraws into the nest that she has carved for herself inside a tree trunk. But even then she doesn't feel quite safe enough, so she seals off the entrance by building a wall of mud. She leaves a tiny opening that's just big enough for her kind and willing partner to pass her food to eat. It's only when her chicks finally hatch that the mother once again ventures outside to look for food. But she always reseals the door behind her until her young are old enough to fly.

THE BEST PROTECTED

The ELF OWL is one of the smallest owls in the world; a child could easily hold it in its hand. The owl is a predator itself, but it's also hunted by many larger animals. It has a small, hooked beak that is of no use for digging a burrow, so it looks for holes made by woodpeckers in huge American cacti. Its enemies, no matter how hungry they might be, are kept away by the cactus's prickles. So, once inside the elf owl can rest in peace.

THE LEAST COMFORTABLE

When winter comes to the North Pole, most Arctic birds migrate to warmer places, but not the ROCK PTARMIGAN. It likes its home too much. In the winter it changes its plumage from brown to white and, when the weather gets impossibly cold, it quickly digs a hole in the snow where it snuggles to keep warm. Throughout the long Arctic winter it has no permanent home. Only when spring comes and the ice begins to melt can it dig a proper nest in the ground and lay its eggs.

THE SMELLIEST

The SCARAB lives in the North African desert and spends its time hunting for animal dung. It carefully rolls the dung into balls (usually much larger than itself) and lays its eggs. Then, it digs a hole in the sand and places the dung balls inside. The balls provide the newborn scarabs with something to eat. Yuck!

THE MOST COMPLEX

The PRAIRIE DOG is a rodent that looks like a very big squirrel, lives in colonies, and digs large complex burrows in the North American prairie. These burrows are impressive, complete with air conditioning, storage rooms, and emergency exits. Some of the colony constantly stand guard outside the burrow and, whenever they catch wind of a coyote or a buzzard, they warn the others by whistling.

THE GREATEST TRESPASSER

The burrows that the prairie dog builds are so large and complex that they often have empty, unused rooms. The BURROWING OWL takes advantage of this and, without so much as a thank you, moves in, saving himself the trouble of having to dig its own burrow. It furnishes its new apartment with dry leaves and turns it into a snug nest for its little ones. Also, the new home comes fully equipped with its own built-in alarm system provided free of charge, of course, by the unsuspecting landlord—the prairie dog.

THE LEAST WELCOME

It's not only the burrowing owl that will visit when uninvited. A RATTLESNAKE will also move into one of the out-of-the-way and lesser-used rooms of another animal's burrow. But it's far from the perfect guest. Unfortunately, it's so mean and deadly that no animal has the courage to try and chase it away. So, it has all the time it needs to make its way around the burrow and eat up its host's babies. What bad manners!

The WART HOG is a wild African pig. It might not look very pretty, but lions and leopards find it an attractive meal. When the pig thinks it's in danger, it uses its feet and tusks to dig a hole in the ground, perhaps enlarging another animal's burrow. Then it hides there anxiously with its whole family until the danger has passed.

THE HASTIEST

FANTASTIC CREATURES

As if not satisfied by nature's cast of characters, people have always devised their own imaginary, extraordinary, or frightening creatures. Some of these are so well known that many people have come to believe that they actually exist. What if they were right after all?

Mokele-Mbembe

Ganesa

The Abominable Snowman

Duck-billed platypus

Chimera

Werewolf

Dragon

Minotaur

Mermaid

The Loch Ness
Monster

THE OLDEST

All civilizations have had their DRAGON, often depicted as a flying reptile that spits fire and carries off young girls. It first appeared about four thousand years ago in China (where it is still revered). Since then, word of the dragon has spread around the world, and it has become part of the folklore of many different cultures. The most striking thing about different descriptions of the dragon is that they all seem remarkably similar to certain kinds of dinosaurs. This may be a coincidence, or perhaps the Chinese had already discovered enormous fossilized bones which had stimulated the imaginations of their storytellers. Or perhaps...?

THE NEWEST

It was only in 1933 that the road was opened that runs all the way around the edge of Loch Ness in Scotland. Immediately, reports began to circulate of sightings of a huge animal with a long neck. THE LOCH NESS MONSTER (nicknamed Nessie by some) quickly became a huge tourist attraction (much encouraged, of course, by the local hotel operators). It has been sighted hundreds of times and often photographed. Several teams of scientists have tried to track it down using sonar and underwater televisions, but they've had no success. Still, they keep on trying.

No dinosaur fossils have ever been found in the Congo. But there are those who claim to have come across a dinosaur-like animal that is still very much alive. Since the last hundred years, explorers who have ventured into the thickest jungle have been shown statues, heard legends, and told eye-witness accounts by the local people of a gigantic reptile which they call MOKELE-MBEMBE. It is very similar to a Sauropod dinosaur, an animal which became extinct millions of years ago.

THE MOST MYSTERIOUS

THE HAIRIEST

Certain species of ancient man also became extinct tens of thousands of years ago. Yet in Tibet and Nepal they tell of a large hairy man-like being that lives alone high up in the glaciers of the Himalayas. THE ABOMINABLE SNOWMAN or YETI (which actually means smelly and not

abominable) has been tracked by numerous explorers. Traces of its existence were found by European mountaineers in the last century, and even Sir Edward Hillary, who conquered Mount Everest, claimed to have seen it. Is this creature really a monkey, a man, or a figment of our imagination? We don't know. There are, in fact, similar legends from all over the world that tell of like beings, sometimes small, sometimes large, and sometimes aggressive, but always hairy.

THE BIGGEST MOVIE STAR

It probably all began long ago in Ancient Greece, when someone saw a man dressed in a wolf-skin coat howling at the moon. This may have developed into the legend of the WEREWOLF, a man who is able to transform himself into a wolf by growing fur, a tail, and large canine teeth. It was the Romans who then carried the story to the rest of Europe. Legends became crowded with descriptions of wolf-men. The cinema has not been able to resist exploiting such a disturbing image and, since 1936, there have been more than fifty films that feature the werewolf.

The MERMAID has also been called upon to appear in numerous films. In the movies, this gorgeous animal—half-fish/half-woman—is loving and sweet. But in the old legends, the mermaid is often described as extremely ugly. Ever since Homer's *Odyssey*, there have been many stories of mermaids who bring nothing but disaster, luring sailors to their deaths so that they could drink their blood.

THE MOST ATTRACTIVE

In Europe the most famous half-man/half-beast is the Minotaur, a half-man/half-bull. According to Greek myth, it was kept by King Minos in a labyrinth on the island of Crete. Being imprisoned certainly didn't do anything to sweeten its temper. It was finally killed by Theseus. Unlike the other fabulous monsters we have discussed, the story of the Minotaur has been imitated. Its fame has been handed down to us unaltered. A true success story!

THE BEST-KNOWN

THE BEST-LOVED

GANESA, half-man/half-elephant (the elephant is a very special animal to Indians), is one of the best-loved of India's six hundred deities. He was the son of Siva and Parvati and protects business people, writers, and scientists. He is red, which is a divine color, and has four hands to symbolize the four realms of consciousness that he controls. He has one good tooth and one broken tooth because he can only see good. He has a huge stomach so that he can digest large quantities of information and he sits astride a mouse, which represents evil. He is adored and his temples are decorated with brilliant colors and huge quantities of flowers are left by his faithful followers.

THE MOST ELABORATE

The Etruscans were an ancient people who lived in Italy. Some 2,500 years ago they made a bronze statue of an animal with the head of an eagle, the shoulders of a lion, the body of a goat, and the tail of a serpent. This was the CHIMERA, a fire-breathing monster that was believed to bring terrible plague and pestilence. When the Etruscans disappeared, the Chimera was forgotten, but the statue still remains as a reminder.

About a hundred years ago, museums in Europe received the first stuffed bodies of an animal with the tail of a beaver, the body of a marmot, and the beak of a duck. When they were told that this creature laid eggs but gave milk to its young and could poison its enemies with one of its nails, they thought they were victims of a hoax. This animal was just too incredible to be real. But it was! The DUCK-BILLED PLATYPUS is still alive today in Australia (though it's now a protected animal and is in danger of becoming extinct).

THE MOST INCREDIBLE

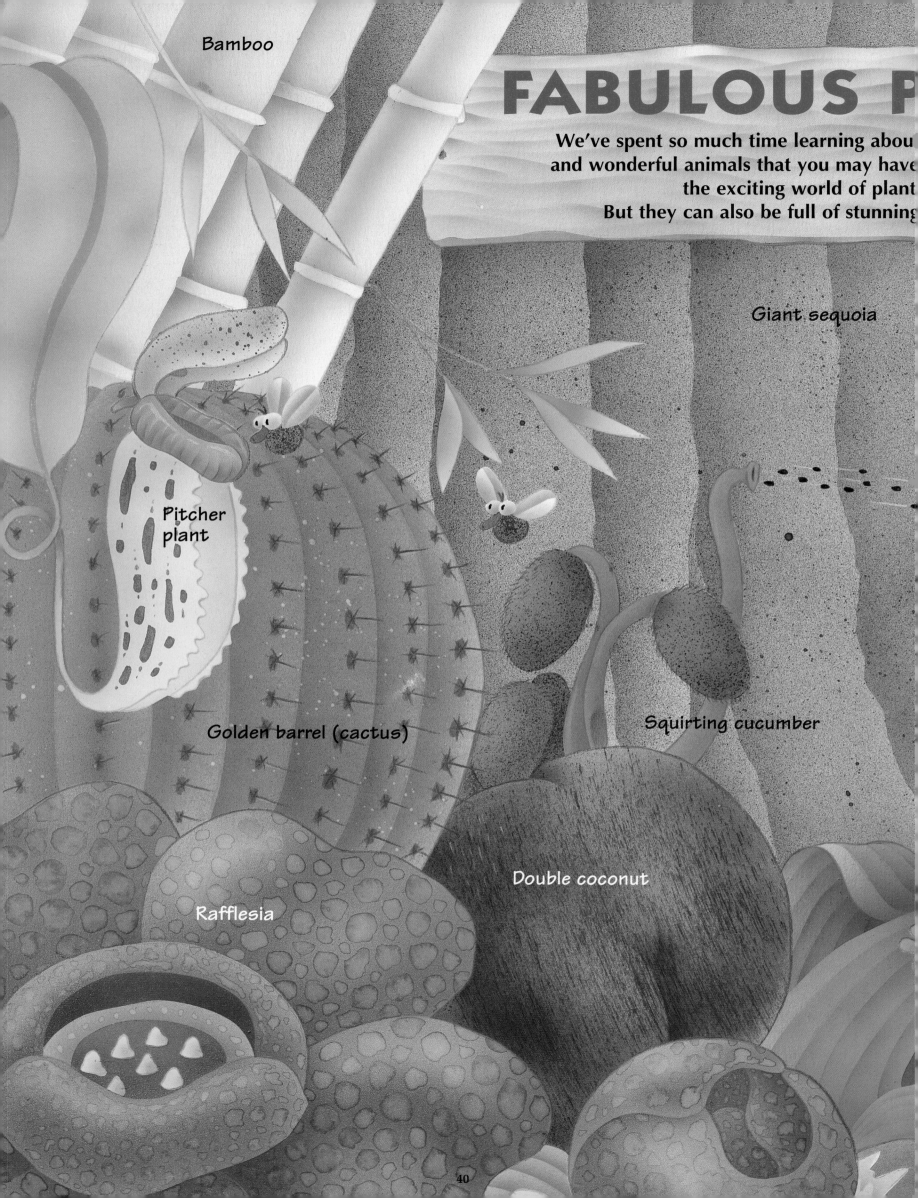

Bamboo

We've spent so much time learning abou
and wonderful animals that you may have
the exciting world of plant
But they can also be full of stunning

Giant sequoia

Pitcher
plant

Golden barrel (cactus)

Squirting cucumber

Double coconut

Rafflesia

40

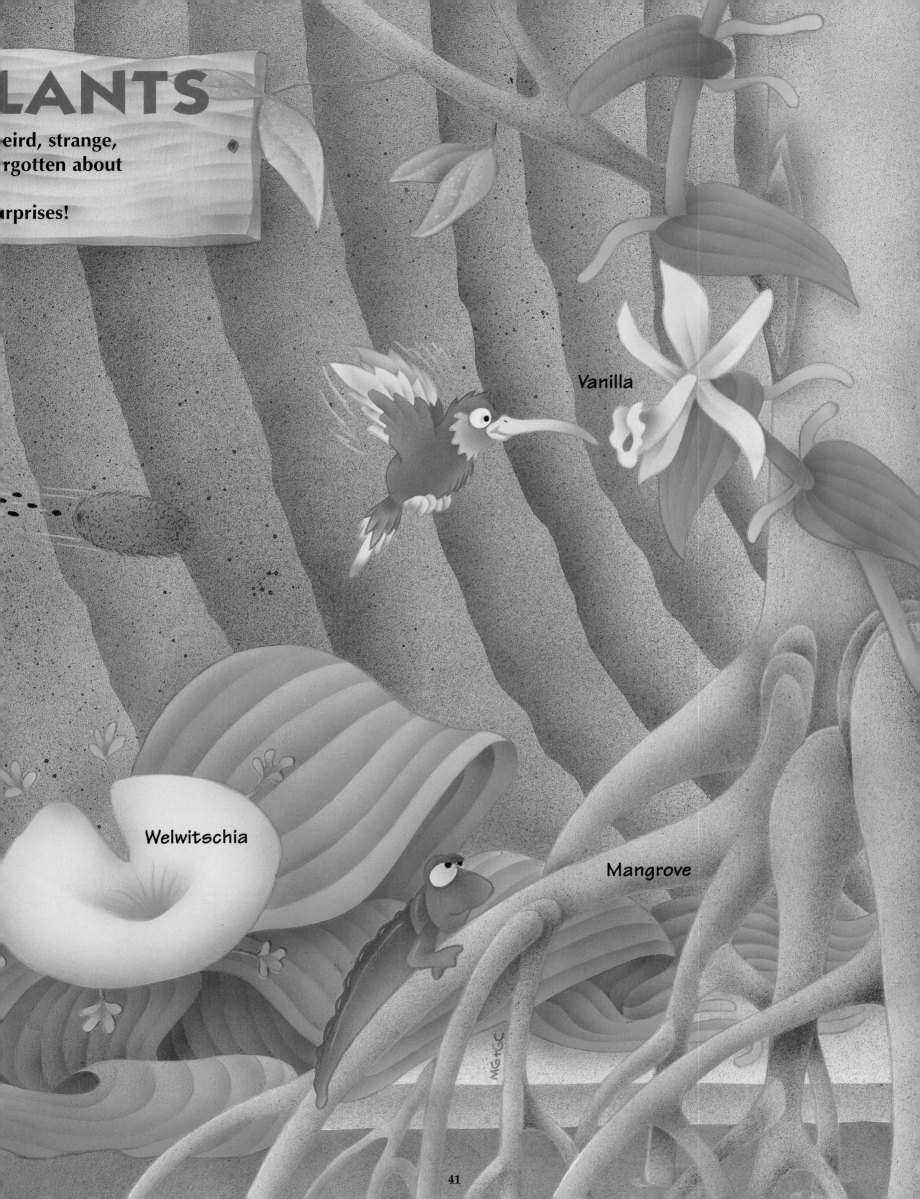

LANTS

eird, strange,
rgotten about

rprises!

Vanilla

Welwitschia

Mangrove

THE BIGGEST

In the American Northwest there grows a tree that weighs more than twenty whales and is as tall as a thirty-story skyscraper. The GIANT SEQUOIA is the most formidable living organism on the face of the Earth, and it's also one of the oldest; some of them are known to be over 1,500 years old.

THE PLUMPEST

Try to imagine a padded footstool as big as your bedroom. The GOLDEN BARREL (its scientific name is ECHINOCACTUS INGENS) may sound like a very comfortable place to sit back and relax, but it's covered with very long spines. The Mexican and North American Indians may not have used it as a stool, but they did use its flesh to make sweets and puddings.

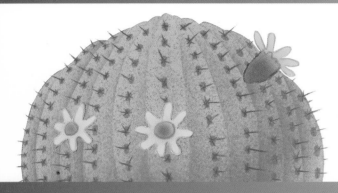

THE MOST EXPLOSIVE

The SQUIRTING CUCUMBER is related to the watermelon and the pumpkin, but it has a unique way of spreading its seeds—it spits them out! The mature fruit contains a pressurized liquid. The slightest tap will cause it to release the liquid and sends it flying more than sixteen yards, leaving a trail of seeds in its wake.

THE SWEETEST

There are many orchids in South America, but one in particular is a favorite—the VANILLA. Its flowers aren't as exotic as some, but its seeds are very special; they can be toasted or ground to make a wonderful powder that has become an essential ingredient in many sweets and ice creams. The vanilla orchid isn't quite as appreciated by other plants in its neighborhood because it's a climbing parasite which, as it grows, gradually suffocates its host plant.

THE SALTIEST

The MANGROVE grows in the tropical lagoons at the mouths of rivers where the muddy river waters mix with salt water from the sea. It's a strange plant whose roots branch out from its trunk lifting it up above the water and making it look as if it were standing on stilts. The word mangrove is a generic name that is used for more than fifty different species of plants. All of them (including the RIZPHORA shown here) are able to withstand a high level of salt in the lagoon water. Indeed, its exposed roots allow it to breathe. They are also much appreciated by the perioftalmo, a little fish that can live out of water and spends a lot of time perched among the mangrove's roots.

THE GREEDIEST

The Indonesian PITCHER PLANT is so-called because its leaves are shaped like a jug. It attracts insects with its bright colors and the perfume of its nectar. This carnivorous plant then eats the insects to obtain the supply of salts and proteins it needs to survive. Any unwary insect that lands on the pitcher plant finds itself in a kind of bag with slippery sides. It slides down into a fatal liquid (a liquid version of quicksand) from which it the bug can't escape.

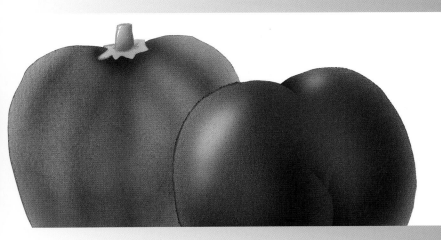

THE MOST ISOLATED

The DOUBLE COCONUT is a plant that lives almost exclusively in the Seychelles, a group of islands in the Indian Ocean. The reason that it's not very widespread is due to the size of its seeds, many of which weigh over twenty-two pounds! They're so heavy that they can't float to far-off lands. However, once polished, these seeds are very attractive and have become quite popular among souvenir-hunting tourists. Now they travel all over the world!

THE MOST FLEXIBLE

The BAMBOO is the world's biggest grass. The DINOCHIOS ANDAMANICA variety can grow to a height of nearly three hundred feet, with stems that are twenty inches in diameter. The BAMBUSA ARUNDINACE grows a record thirty-five inches a day. Because bamboo bends easily, an incredible number of uses have been found for it. It's used to create everything from fishing rods to works of art and even buildings.

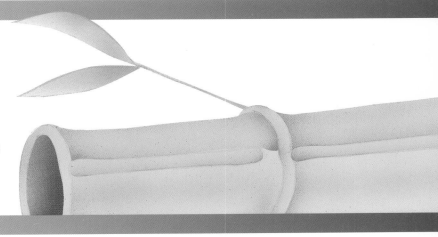

THE MOST OVERWHELMING

In the Namibian desert in southern Africa you'll find the WELWITSCHIA. It grows along the ground and has only two leaves, each of which can easily reach a length of more than fifty feet. They are the only leaves in the plant world that continue growing throughout their lives, getting ever longer and more frayed, and ending up looking like flat spaghetti. The plant can live for more than one thousand years, so it can end up covering quite a lot of ground.

THE SMELLIEST

If you've ever enjoyed sniffing a flower with a highly intense perfume, try to think what it might smell like if the flower were the size of a large umbrella! The RAFFLESIA is the world's biggest flower. Unfortunately, the rafflesia stinks of decaying meat. When the flower is merely a bud, it's the same size as a football. Yet, surprisingly enough, the plant it grows from is a slender parasite which lives on the lianas of the Indonesian forests.

ACKNOWLEDGEMENTS

As in other books of mine, the realization of the texts would not have been possible
without the brilliant and expert help of Giorgio Chiozzo,
an illustrator and biologist from the Museum of Natural History of Milan.
Laura Adai has, with incredible patience,
helped me in the lengthy task of coloring the plates,
and the editorial team at Dodo has encouraged and supported me throughout the process.
It's thanks to them that the book you are now holding in your hands
was finally able to see the light of day.

A very big *thank you* to all.

ANIMAL INDEX